OPIUM WARS

A History from Beginning to End

Copyright © 2018 by Hourly History.

Table of Contents

Introduction

Armed groups fighting for the control of a lucrative and illegal narcotics trade is something we commonly associate with organized crime and the underworld of large modern cities. But it hasn't always been like that. In the nineteenth century, two of the world's most powerful nations went to war over illegal narcotics. One fought for the right to keep these drugs out of their country. The other fought for the right to supply the increasing numbers of people who were hopelessly addicted.

Great Britain's wars with China over the supply of opium to Chinese addicts was one of the most shameful episodes of British Imperialism, referred to by no less a figure than William Gladstone as wars "calculated to cover this country with permanent disgrace." The outcome of these wars was victory for Britain, the virtual destruction of China as a world power, and the creation of millions of drug addicts.

Just how did this happen? How did a country which boasted of the "glorious traditions of the British Flag" come to fight a war not just on behalf of drug smugglers, but in order to force a sovereign nation to accept their pernicious trade? This is the story of the Opium Wars.

Chapter One

The Joy Plant

"Of all the remedies it has pleased almighty God to give man to relieve his suffering, none is so universal and so efficacious as opium."

—Thomas Sydenham

Opium is almost as old as human civilization. The Sumerians, the mysterious people who settled in ancient Mesopotamia many thousands of years ago, were known to cultivate the *Hul Gil* ("joy plant"), and this knowledge was passed on to the Assyrians, the Babylonians, the Egyptians, the Greeks, and the Romans. Early users of opium either ate or drank mixtures containing opium, mainly for medicinal purposes. It wasn't until the 1500s that Portuguese sailors on ships trading in the East China Sea began the recreational smoking of this drug, producing a much more intense and virtually instant effect.

In 1600, Queen Elizabeth granted a charter to a new English trading company, the Governor and Company of Merchants of London trading with the East Indies. This company, which became better known as the East India Company, provided trade between Britain, India, and Asia. One of the commodities brought back to England by the new company was high-quality opium from India. After 1756, when the British conquered Calcutta, the heartland of

Indian opium production, the export of opium from India became big business for the East India Company.

Opium became popular for medicinal purposes in Britain and formed an element of many popular sleeping potions and other medicines including laudanum, an alcoholic herbal mixture containing powdered opium. Laudanum became so popular as a painkiller and sleep aid that it has been called the "aspirin of the nineteenth century." Other medicines which contained opium became very popular in Britain and Europe and were recommended for everything from relieving pain to curing diarrhea, preventing depression, and promoting restful sleep. There was even a popular children's medicine, Godfrey's Cordial, which contained treacle, water, and opium. This concoction was recommended for colic, hiccups, and coughs. Opium-based medicines were widely available, not just from pharmacists but also in tobacconists, wine merchants, stationers, and even barbers.

But it didn't take long for it to become apparent that there were some notable problems with the use of opium-based medicines. The most significant was addiction—by the late 1700s, people were discovering that it was much easier to begin taking the drug than it was to stop. For example, the poet Samuel Taylor Coleridge started taking laudanum as a young man following a painful bout of rheumatic fever. He became completely addicted, writing to a friend: "I was seduced into the ACCURSED Habit ignorantly—I had been almost bed ridden for many months with swelling in my knees—in a medical journal I happily met with an account of a cure performed in a similar case . . . by rubbing in of Laudanum, at the same time taking a given dose internally—it acted like a charm, like a miracle!"

Writers who used laudanum included Charles Dickens, Elizabeth Barrett Browning, and George Eliot in addition to other poets including Percy Bysshe Shelley and John Keats. In 1821, Thomas De Quincey, a friend of Coleridge, published *Confessions of an English Opium-Eater* in serial form in the *London Magazine*. This detailed his use of laudanum and other opium-based drugs. The early parts extolled the virtue of opium, though later parts also described De Quincey's battles with addiction. By 1830, the importation of opium into England reached its peak with a total of 22,000 pounds of opium being brought into the country in that year.

However, sensationalized accounts of opium dens in fiction and non-fiction in the mid-nineteenth century confirmed the growing belief that opium wasn't the harmless medicine it was sometimes portrayed as. Gradually, people in Victorian England began to turn against opium, though it wouldn't be until 1868 and the introduction of the Pharmacy Act that the unregulated sale of opium-based products would finally be addressed.

The dwindling market for opium in Britain posed a particular problem for the East India Company, a substantial portion of whose profits came from the importation of opium produced in India. From 1800, the East India Company had a complete monopoly on opium produced in India—poppy growers were barred from selling their product to anyone but accredited representatives of the company. The company had already established trade routes smuggling opium into China where the Dutch had introduced the locals to the smoking of opium in pipes in the eighteenth century.

Opium had become such a problem in China that Emperor Yung Cheng issued an imperial edict in 1729 specifically forbidding the smoking of opium, though it was still allowed to be used for medicinal purposes. The prohibition had little effect, however, causing Emperor Kia King to make all use and trade of opium illegal in China in 1799. Even this had little effect as the East India Company simply auctioned opium to smugglers and independent traders who then transported it into China for enormous profits. The East India Company was paid in silver, which helped to offset a massive trade imbalance between Great Britain and China.

The demand for Chinese exports, especially tea, silk, and porcelain, was huge in Britain, but there were few British products that interested the Chinese. All exports from China therefore had to be paid for in silver, and this meant a substantial trade deficit for Britain as silver flowed into China. The opium trade conducted by the East India Company helped to rebalance this deficit and became an important part of Britain's trade with Asia. In the early 1800s, over 1,000 tons of opium each year were being sold to middlemen in Canton who smuggled the drug into mainland China. Thus, the trade deficit was turned into a surplus.

The effects of the illicit importation of opium into China were becoming very serious indeed by the early 1830s. It has been estimated that up to 90% of the male population in some coastal areas of China were addicted to smoking opium—this represented about 12 million people.

Overall, up to one-fourth of the male population in China were thought to be addicted to opium. Naturally this had devastating social consequences, and the Chinese leadership began to look for ways of tackling the problem.

A court official described the effect that opium smoking was having: "At the beginning, opium smoking was confined to the fops of wealthy families who took up the habit as a form of conspicuous consumption, even they knew that they should not indulge in it to the greatest extreme. Later, people of all social strata—from government officials and members of the gentry to craftsmen, merchants, entertainers, and servants, and even women, Buddhist monks and nuns, and Taoist priests—took up the habit and openly bought and equipped themselves with smoking instruments."

It wasn't just British traders that recognized the potential in the opium trade. American traders began buying opium in Turkey and importing it into China—for example, Warren Delano, grandfather of future U.S. President Franklin Delano Roosevelt, became wealthy as a result of trading opium into China. The Turkish opium was cheaper than Indian opium, which led to prices dropping in China and more people becoming addicted to the drug. Other European traders also became involved in the trade with opium from several sources.

Part of the problem in tackling opium smoking was that the Qing government, located in Beijing in the north of China, was physically distant from the southern coastal provinces where the problem of opium addiction was most acute. Edicts issued by the government simply had less force in the south, and large numbers of customs and other officials were receiving substantial bribes. Some members of the imperial court suggested accepting that the trade in opium existed and taxing it, providing revenue which could then be used to suppress the use of the drug. However, the Daoguang Emperor, eighth emperor of the Manchu Qing dynasty, disagreed. Instead, he sent a member of his court who was totally opposed to the use and trade in opium, Lin Zexu, to the southern provinces to tackle the problem. To ensure that he had sufficient authority to effectively undertake this task, the emperor appointed Lin Zexu as imperial commissioner, a position that carried power second only to that of the emperor himself. Lin Zexu was empowered to negotiate directly with foreign powers and to take whatever steps he felt necessary to end the opium trade.

Chapter Two

Outbreak of the First Opium War

"Our Celestial Empire possesses all things in prolific abundance and lacks no product within its borders. There is therefore no need to import the manufactures of outside barbarians in exchange for our own produce."

—Qianlong Emperor of China

When Lin Zexu arrived in Canton (the only Chinese port open to foreign traders) in March of 1839, he proceeded to tackle the opium problem in the most direct way possible. He issued an edict instructing all British merchants there to hand over any stocks of opium they held. They were given three days to oblige, and the penalty for refusing to cooperate was death. The British superintendent of trade in Canton, Charles Elliot, attempted to negotiate with Lin Zexu who responded by suspending all foreign trade with China and taking hostage all British merchants in Canton by confining them to their factories and cutting off supplies. Faced with no option, the merchants handed over all their stocks of opium, which amounted to over 1,200 tons. These were promptly destroyed in public on a beach outside Canton. Chinese troops also boarded British ships in the South China Sea and on the Pearl River, confiscating and destroying any opium that they found.

The British government was outraged. Not only had a lucrative trade been cut off completely, but private property belonging to British subjects had also been confiscated and destroyed. To confirm that he intended to end the opium trade once and for all, Lin Zexu sent a letter to Queen Victoria in which he noted that: "Your Majesty has not before been thus officially notified, and you may plead ignorance of the severity of our laws, but I now give my assurance that we mean to cut this harmful drug forever." Lin Zexu issued an edict banning all further import of opium and threatening the death penalty for anyone, including foreign merchants, who were found to be involved.

Tensions ran high between the Chinese authorities and foreign merchants in Canton. Then, in July 1839, a group of British sailors enjoying shore leave in Kowloon, a port near Hong Kong, drank rather too much rice wine. They then became involved in an argument with a local man, Lin Weixi, who they proceeded to beat to death. Superintendent of Trade Charles Elliot had the two sailors said to be responsible for the murder arrested, and compensation was paid to the family of Lin Weixi. Lin Zexu was not satisfied with these actions and demanded that the men be handed over to the Chinese authorities to stand trial. Elliot refused, and the sailors were tried on a British ship and sentenced to periods of hard labor in Britain (though these sentences would later be overturned when the men returned to England). Lin Zexu responded by banning the sale of food to British merchants or ships and deploying war junks to the mouth of the Pearl River where they could control access to Canton.

In late August 1839, a ship operated by a British merchant who was known to have been involved in smuggling opium was attacked by pirates in the South China Sea. Rumors spread amongst the British that this was a covert attack carried out by the Chinese navy and authorized by Lin Zexu. Concerned, Elliot ordered all British ships to leave Chinese ports and banned British trade with China until the threat of the death penalty for merchants dealing in opium was lifted. By the end of August, over 60 British ships with more than 2,000 people aboard were anchored off the Coast of China with limited supplies of food and water. On August 30, a Royal Navy sailing frigate, HMS *Volage*, arrived to protect the British ships.

On September 4, Elliot sent an armed schooner accompanied by a cutter into the port of Kowloon to buy supplies for the British ships. The harbor was protected by three war junks which allowed the British ships to pass. The British were provided with basic necessities but were prohibited from trading with the locals by the Chinese commander of the Kowloon fort. Dissatisfied, Elliot issued an ultimatum—either the Chinese provided supplies or the British ships would open fire. At three o'clock that afternoon, the British ships opened fire on the war junks and the fort. Both returned fire, and the exchange of shots continued until darkness fell. At that point the Chinese war junks withdrew, and Elliot was able to bribe local merchants to provide supplies. He also had a paper printed which was circulated in Kowloon. It read: "The men of the

English nation desire nothing but peace; but they cannot submit to be poisoned and starved. The Imperial cruizers they have no wish to molest or impede; but they must not prevent the people from selling. To deprive men of food is the act only of the unfriendly and hostile." When they had obtained the required supplies, the two British ships left Kowloon and returned to where the other British ships were at anchor.

The commander of Kowloon fort issued a communiqué announcing a great victory over the British in the Battle of Kowloon. Two British warships had been sunk, he claimed, and many British sailors killed. Most importantly, he told his superiors that the British had been prevented from obtaining any supplies in Kowloon. The truth was that no British ships had been sunk or even seriously damaged, no British sailors had been killed, and the British had been able to obtain all the supplies they wanted. This habit of local commanders issuing triumphant communiqués which bore little relation to reality was to be a notable feature of the coming conflict.

Then, in October 1839, a British merchant ship, the *Thomas Coutts*, arrived in Canton. The owners of the ship were Quakers who had always refused to take part in the opium trade, something that was known to the Chinese authorities. The *Thomas Coutts* unloaded its cargo in Canton, defying Elliot's instruction that all trade with China was to be suspended.

On November 3, a second Quaker-owned British merchant ship, the *Royal Saxon*, attempted to sail up the Pearl River to Canton. Two Royal Navy ships patrolling in the area fired warning shots at the *Royal Saxon*, and several

Chinese war junks sailed down the river to investigate. The exchange of fire which followed became known as the First Battle of Chuenpi. The Chinese war junks protecting the *Royal Saxon* proved to be almost completely ineffective in battle—one was blown up, three were sunk, and several more were seriously damaged while the British ships virtually escaped damage, though one British sailor was slightly wounded. The Chinese war vessels withdrew to Canton, and the *Royal Saxon* followed. The official Chinese report of the action noted another great victory against the British. This odd little battle, where British ships opened fire against a British merchant ship is by some viewed as the official beginning of the First Opium War as opposed to the Battle of Kowloon on September 4.

Concerned about the possibility of further Chinese attacks, Elliot moved his fleet to an anchorage 20 miles from the Portuguese-controlled island of Macau. He hoped to be able to obtain supplies there, but on January 14, 1840, the Chinese emperor issued an edict forbidding all foreign merchants in China from providing supplies to the British. Fearing that he might be cut off from vital Chinese supplies, the governor of Macau refused to provide any assistance to the British ships.

In Britain, the situation in China was causing concern. During her annual address to the House of Lords, Queen Victoria noted: "Events have happened in China which have occasioned an interruption of the commercial intercourse of my subjects with that country. I have given, and shall continue to give, the most serious attention to a matter so deeply affecting the interests of my subjects and the dignity of my Crown." The Whig government under the leadership of Prime Minister William Melbourne was generally in favor of war, especially the bellicose foreign secretary, Henry John Temple, 3rd Viscount Palmerston. In February 1840, Palmerston ordered a British force to be prepared for dispatch to China and sent a letter to the Chinese emperor warning him that British naval and military forces were on the way: "These measures of hostility on the part of Great Britain against China are not only justified, but even rendered absolutely necessary, by the outrages which have been committed by the Chinese Authorities against British officers and Subjects, and these hostilities will not cease, until a satisfactory arrangement shall have been made by the Chinese Government."

The British government was opposed in its desire for war by both the Tory and Liberal parties, but in a debate in Parliament in 1840, it was agreed that Britain would go to war with China, ostensibly to uphold the principles of free trade but in reality to protect the lucrative British narcotics trade. The war was not planned as a full-scale invasion of China, but rather as a punitive expedition which would attack Chinese ports and military installations in order to force the Chinese to accede to British demands, which included not just the restitution of the opium trade but the payment of compensation for the opium which had been confiscated and destroyed on the orders of Lin Zexu.

While the British assembled their forces in Singapore, Elliot withdrew his small fleet to safer waters, though British warships continued to patrol off the Pearl River.

Chapter Three

British Superiority and the Devil Ship

"All we wanted might have been got, if it had not been for the unaccountably strange conduct of Charles Elliot."

—Queen Victoria

In June 1840, the British Expeditionary Force left Singapore for China under the command of Commodore Gordon Bremer, an experienced naval officer who had seen combat in the Napoleonic Wars. The force included four steam gunboats, fifteen barrack-ships which contained Royal Marines trained in amphibious landing, and a great many smaller ships.

The British began the campaign by attacking Zhoushan Island in the Zhoushan Archipelago. This island included the port of Dinghai, a vital staging area for the planned British operations. Zhoushan was protected by Chinese naval units comprising large numbers of war junks, but these were easily defeated when the British launched their initial attack at the beginning of July. The port city of Dinghai was captured following a naval bombardment on July 5.

The British force was then divided into two fleets. One went south to the Pearl River while the other went north to the Yellow Sea. Charles Elliot, who had been given full authority to negotiate on behalf of the British government, went with the northern fleet. Elliot landed at Peiho in northeastern China where he was able to meet Qishan, a new official appointed by the emperor to negotiate with the British following the dismissal of Lin Zexu. After a week of negotiations, Qishan agreed that imperial funds would be used to compensate British merchants whose opium had been confiscated if the British agreed to withdraw from the Yellow Sea. It was also agreed that further discussions would be conducted on the Pearl River.

In the meantime, British naval forces strengthened by reinforcements from Singapore had attacked Macau Island. These included the first British Army unit to join the expedition, the 37th Madras Native Infantry, and a new and terrifying weapon: HMS *Nemesis*. The *Nemesis* was the first British warship constructed of iron (and one of the first steam-powered, iron warships in the world), and the Chinese war junks were helpless against this new technology. The *Nemesis* quickly became known as the "Devil Ship" to the Chinese navy. In late August 1840, the *Nemesis* and two other British warships supported by over 300 Royal Navy Marines attacked Macau and quickly took the island. With ports in Macau and Dinghai secured, the British were free to reinforce and to plan their attack on the Pearl River and the port of Canton.

The Chinese defenders had established strong positions in Humen at the mouth of the Pearl River which protected the approaches to Canton. The forts at Humen were occupied by more than 3,000 soldiers and protected by some 300 heavy cannons, and there were also heavy artillery batteries on Chuenpi Island. In early January 1841, British warships began to bombard the forts at Humen. On January 7 at around 08:00, a total of over 1,000 British troops supported by units of the Royal Artillery were landed near Chinese artillery batteries on Chuenpi Island. British warships including the *Nemesis* bombarded the defenses while the troops attacked, and within two hours Chuenpi Island was in British hands. The Chinese responded by sending a group of 15 heavily armed war junks to engage the British warships. The *Nemesis* attacked the junks, and in a short battle 11 were destroyed and the remainder abandoned.

The capture of Chuenpi Island in what became known as the Second Battle of Chuenpi meant that the British controlled the approach to Canton and Chinese naval units retreated up the Pearl River towards the city. The following day the British had intended to attack the remaining forts, but an envoy appeared bearing a message from Imperial Commissioner Qishan who asked for a ceasefire to allow negotiations with Charles Elliot. This was agreed, and Elliot and Qishan spent several days in discussion. Finally, on January 20, 1841, an agreement was announced: Under the Convention of Chuenpi, Britain would be given Hong Kong, a six million silver dollar indemnity to recompense for the opium destroyed on Lin Zexu's orders, and trade in Canton would be reopened with no mention of the death penalty for opium smugglers.

This convention pleased no-one, however, and both the British and Chinese governments refused to sign it. The emperor ordered Qishan stripped of his office; he was to return to Beijing to face trial at the Board of Punishments, charged amongst other things with giving "the barbarians Hong Kong as a dwelling place." Qishan was found guilty and sentenced to death, though this sentence was not carried out and he was instead imprisoned. Charles Elliot fared a little better. Palmerston wrote him a letter of reprimand complaining that the convention he had agreed did not secure the British opium trade and noting that Hong Kong was "a barren island with hardly a house upon it." Queen Victoria was also severely displeased with Elliot. In a letter she noted that Elliot "completely disobeyed his instructions and tried to get the lowest terms he could." It was decided that Elliot should be dismissed from his post and replaced as superintendent of trade by Sir Henry Pottinger. Pottinger, however, would not arrive in China until August 1841.

Even while Pottinger was en route, fighting broke out once again between British and Chinese forces. While negotiations between Elliot and Qishan were taking place, both sides had observed an unofficial truce, and the British had lifted their blockade of the Pearl River. Elliot, who was still in command at this point and unaware that he had been dismissed, expected that the peace treaty agreed with Qishan would be accepted by both sides. Soon it became evident that the Chinese were using the truce to strengthen the fortifications in the remaining forts on the Pearl River, and Commodore Bremer began to suspect (correctly) that the Chinese had no intention of signing the treaty and were instead stalling for time as they improved their defenses.

On February 19, a longboat from HMS *Nemesis* was said to have been fired upon on by one of the Chinese forts on North Wangtong Island. The British blockade was immediately reimposed, and on February 23, British naval units attacked Chinese forts on North Wangtong and Anunghoy islands. The outcome was a decisive victory for the British. By February 26, both islands were occupied, more than 300 Chinese cannons were captured, and a large number of Chinese war junks had been destroyed. Chinese casualties were around 500 killed (including Admiral Guan Tianpei, commander-in-chief of Chinese naval forces in the area) and an unknown number of wounded. Total British casualties were five wounded.

The following day, on February 27, British units attacked the last remaining Chinese fort in the area on First Bar Island. The result was another rout—over 300 Chinese were killed, and a large number of cannons were captured. British casualties were one killed (accidentally shot himself with his own musket) and eight wounded. It was becoming very clear that Chinese military and naval units were no match for the well-trained British forces equipped with the latest weapons. The only modern warship in the Chinese navy, the former East India ship *Cambridge*, was sunk during this battle.

With the capture of First Bar Island, the British had complete control of the lower Pearl River and began to make plans to advance upriver towards Canton. By the time Qishan's replacement, the emperor's cousin Yishan, arrived in Canton in mid-April to resume negotiations with Elliot, the British had already occupied parts of the city. While these negotiations were continuing, the Chinese defenses around Canton were strengthened—more than 50,000 troops were stationed around the city, additional artillery batteries were emplaced, and large numbers of small ships were provided with cannons. The emperor issued an edict demanding that the people of Canton "exterminate the rebels at all points." This proved to be more difficult than anticipated.

On the night of May 21, 1841, hidden artillery batteries opened fire on British warships in the vicinity of Canton, many small boats engaged British ships, and over 200 fire rafts were sent down the river in an effort to set fire to the British ships. Not one British ship was seriously damaged, and on May 25, Major General Gough, the commander of British land forces, launched an assault on Canton. By May 30, the city was completely occupied by British forces, and all the defending Chinese troops had fled into the surrounding countryside.

However, Elliot then signed a peace treaty with Yishan in which the British were paid a substantial sum to leave the city and withdraw back down the Pearl River, something that angered the British naval and military commanders who had not been consulted before the treaty was signed. Yishan used this opportunity to send a letter to the emperor noting that the British had begged "that he would have mercy upon them, and cause their debts to be repaid them, and graciously permit them to carry on their commerce, when they would immediately withdraw their ships from the Bocca Tigris, and never dare again to raise any disturbance."

Under the misapprehension that British forces on the Pearl River had been defeated, the emperor planned for the completion of the war by ejecting the British entirely from China. Following the withdrawal from Canton, the British relocated to Hong Kong and began to plan for the next stage of the assault on China.

Chapter Four

The Treaty of Nanking: First of the Unequal Treaties

"The British seizure of Hong Kong was an aspect of one of the most ugly crimes of the British Empire: the takeover and destruction of India, and the use of India to flood China with opium."

—Robert Trout

In Hong Kong, the British debated the next move. Charles Elliot wanted to end the war and to reestablish normal trade between Britain and China. His military commanders disagreed strongly, telling him that they should continue the war until the Chinese were prepared to accept all British demands. This impasse continued until July 29, 1841, when Elliot finally discovered that he was to be replaced. The new Superintendent of trade, Sir Henry Pottinger, arrived on August 10 and it quickly became clear that he was much more belligerent than Elliot. He instructed the expeditionary force to go ahead with its war plans, and on August 21, the British fleet left Hong Kong bound for the city of Amoy, an important port on the Taiwan Strait.

The British fleet arrived at the mouth of the Jiulong River on August 25 and proceeded to attack Amoy on the 26th. The defenses of the city had been well prepared, but Royal Marines and infantry units supported by fire from warships stormed the city, and the following day it was in British hands. Many war junks were destroyed, over 100 cannons were captured, and the city's defenders fled. The British forces then withdrew to an island on the Jiulong River where they built a fort which was able to blockade the river completely. After British forces had withdrawn, Chinese troops cautiously re-entered the city. The governor then sent the emperor a message claiming that the British attack had been successfully repulsed and five British warships sunk.

In October 1841, British forces captured the ports of Zhoushan and Ningbo before settling in for the winter to rest and resupply. In late 1841, the Chinese emperor finally realized that he had been receiving reports of the fighting with the British that were, to say the least, optimistic. Until then, the emperor had believed that his troops were winning; now, he realized that this was completely untrue. As a result, Yishan was recalled to the capital where he was tried by the imperial court. He was then removed from command. Aware now of the scale of the threat, the emperor ordered that all coastal cities should prepare to repulse British attacks.

In March 1842, the emperor ordered another relative, Prince Yijing, to recapture Ningbo. The attack on British defenders was carried out with great courage and an almost complete lack of success. Chinese troops suffered heavy casualties during a number of fruitless frontal attacks.

On May 18, the British captured the important port city of Zhapu. The capture of Zhapu and Ningbo gave British forces access to the vital Yangtze River. A British fleet of 25 warships carrying over 10,000 troops sailed up the river and almost immediately captured the emperor's tax barges leading to an immediate shortage of money for the imperial court.

On June 14, the mouth of the Huangpu River, a tributary of the Yangtze, was captured by the British. The fleet sailed up the Huangpu, and by June 19, British forces had captured the cities of Wusong, Baoshan, and Shanghai. On July 14, the British fleet resumed its journey up the Yangtze; this time its target was the city of Chinkiang, a vital strategic asset. Chinkiang controlled access to the city of Nanking, but it was also near the confluence of the Grand Canal and the Yangtze River. These two major waterways comprised the bulk of the Caoyun system which allowed the distribution of grain throughout China. If Chinkiang was lost, the Chinese Empire would be effectively crippled.

The British attacked Chinkiang on July 21, 1842. Chinese forts were destroyed by fire from warships, and then British troops were landed. They stormed the city; more than 30 British soldiers and Marines were killed during bitter street fighting, the highest casualties suffered by the British during any engagement during the First Opium War. Despite this, the city was taken before nightfall. On August 3, the British fleet sailed on up the Yangtze with the intention of taking the city of Nanking. However, when the fleet arrived off Nanking about one week later, they were met by a delegation from the imperial court who wished to negotiate a peace treaty.

What became known as the Treaty of Nanking was signed on August 29, 1842, officially ending the First Opium War. This treaty gave the British the island of Hong Kong and a six million silver dollars indemnity in recompense for the destruction of opium in Canton, three million dollars to recompensate for debts, and twelve million dollars for the cost of war. The largest gain for the British, however, were the sweeping changes which would be implemented to foreign trade in China—new ports would be opened to foreign trade, the Cohong monopoly would be abolished, and foreigners would be allowed to trade with anyone they wished. It was notable that the treaty did not explicitly define the rights of British merchants in regards to opium. The British assumed that this would be clarified in subsequent treaties, but this was to prove more complicated and more challenging than anyone had thought.

One thing which surprised the British almost as much as their Chinese adversaries was the ease with which British forces triumphed in virtually every action in the First Opium War. A major factor in this was the superiority of the weapons and tactics used by the British. In terms of naval units, for example, the Chinese tended to employ large numbers of war junks, unarmored sailing craft carrying up to ten fixed cannons. However, the Chinese cannons were of inferior quality to those provided on British warships and capable of accuracy at much shorter range. The British warships were more maneuverable (and the most modern steamships like HMS *Nemesis* could sail against the wind and tide, something the war junks were unable to do) and could destroy ships from long ranges from which the Chinese ships were unable to fire back. The British ships also carried more cannons than the Chinese junks—large ships like HMS *Cornwallis* carried more cannons than a whole fleet of war junks. The same thing applied to the cannons on the many river forts constructed by the Chinese. Although on paper these looked like formidable defenses, British ships were able to fire accurately from beyond the range of Chinese guns, destroying the forts and their cannons which were not able to fire back.

On land, Chinese forces also faced superior weaponry. British soldiers were equipped with Brunswick rifles or Brown Bess muskets modified with rifled barrels. These were accurate at up to 300 meters compared to little more than 100 meters for the elderly matchlock muskets used by the majority of Chinese infantry. Many of the British weapons also used percussion caps, a relatively new invention which made these weapons less prone to misfire in damp weather, something that was a constant problem with the Chinese matchlocks. Due to improved forging techniques, British artillery was much lighter than Chinese weapons, meaning that it could more easily and quickly be moved into position than the heavier Chinese guns. British artillery was also more accurate at longer ranges than Chinese guns, all of which contributed to the ability of British forces to defeat larger Chinese armies.

British strategy and tactics were also superior. Naval captains and commanders of even small infantry units were encouraged to use a high degree of initiative to respond to changing battlefield conditions. Chinese military and naval units were under very strict control from above at all times, which meant that changing tactics in response to changing conditions was virtually impossible. This lack of flexibility on the part of Chinese forces proved to be disastrous in the type of fast-moving modern warfare which characterized the First Opium War.

Chapter Five

The Inevitable Second Opium War

"A war more unjust in its origin, a war more calculated to cover this country with permanent disgrace, I do not know, and I have not read of."

—William Gladstone

In Canton, acts of aggression against British subjects continued after the signing of the Treaty of Nanking and the resumption of trade. These became so serious that in April 1847, the governor of Hong Kong, Sir John Davis, demanded compensation from Qiying, one of the Chinese commissioners who had negotiated the Treaty of Nanking. Unsatisfied by the response, Davis ordered Major-General George D'Aguilar, the new commander-in-chief of British forces in China, to prepare to occupy Canton.

A fleet of British warships approached the forts at the mouth of the Pearl River on April 2, 1847, and Anunghoy Island, North Wangtong Island, and South Wangtong Island were bombarded and quickly occupied. The British fleet then sailed up the river and captured the remaining ten forts guarding the approaches to Canton. The British suffered no casualties during this operation (which became known as the Expedition to Canton) while nearly 900

Chinese cannons were captured, leaving Canton with virtually no effective defenses against a British invasion. With no alternative, Commissioner Qiying agreed to ensure that the people who had committed aggressive acts towards British merchants would be punished and that compensation would be paid.

Although it officially wasn't part of a war, the Expedition to Canton proved once again British military supremacy and emphasized the weakness of the Qing dynasty. However, China remained a potentially huge source of trade, and Britain wasn't the only country interested in exploiting this. In 1844, the Chinese authorities had signed the Treaty of Whampoa with the French. This gave French traders essentially the same privileges as the British had received under the Treaty of Nanking just two years earlier. The treaty did not please the British who had assumed that their military successes against the Chinese would give them most favored nation status in trade with China. Also in 1844, China signed the Treaty of Wanghia with the United States. This, in British eyes, was even worse because it not only guaranteed America equal trading rights with Britain but also gave them the right to buy land in five nominated Chinese ports.

Both these new treaties contained clauses that allowed them to be renegotiated after 12 years. Although no such clause had been included in the Treaty of Nanking, the British immediately began to pressure the Chinese to agree to a new version of this treaty. The British wanted the new treaty to include, amongst other things, permission for British merchants to trade in all areas of China, legalization of the opium trade, and English-language versions of treaties to take precedence over Chinese versions. The opium trade was a particular source of concern to the British. The Treaty of Nanking had not addressed it at all, and the importation of opium into China was technically illegal, though it was still taking place on a huge scale. Its illegality meant that the Chinese authorities could decide to clamp down on this lucrative trade at any time.

The Chinese remained extremely concerned about levels of opium addiction and refused to consider making trade in this narcotic legal. The argument with the British over the renegotiation of the Treaty of Nanking rumbled on throughout the early 1850s without anything being decided. Then, on October 8, 1856, Chinese troops seized the *Arrow*, a merchant ship flying the British flag in Canton harbor and arrested twelve of its Chinese crew on suspicion of being pirates. The *Arrow* had certainly been operating as a pirate ship in the past, but it had been re-registered as a British vessel in Hong Kong and it had a British master, Captain Thomas Kennedy. Kennedy had not been aboard the Arrow at the time it was seized, but he reported the incident to the British consul in Canton, Sir Harry Parkes. Parkes demanded the immediate release of the ship and the arrested crew members.

The Chinese authorities released nine of the arrested crew members, but refused to release the last three, maintaining that they were pirates. The British reacted in typical fashion on October 23 by bringing in warships and bombarding forts on the river before beginning a bombardment of the city of Canton itself. The British occupied the city and remained in control until January 5, 1857 when they withdrew to Hong Kong following the completion of negotiations, though the last three members of the *Arrow* crew were not released.

There seems little doubt that the refusal of the Chinese authorities to release the arrested crew members would have led to more conflict with the British if the Indian Mutiny had not broken out in 1857. This was a large-scale rebellion against the rule of the East India Company in India which required large numbers of troops to suppress, meaning that military forces could not be spared for action in China. However, the death of a French missionary gave the French an excuse to begin their own military action against the Chinese.

Father Auguste Chapdelaine was a French Catholic missionary working in China on behalf of the Paris Foreign Missions Society. Missionaries had managed to convert small numbers of local people to the Catholic faith in various parts of China. In some parts of China this was permitted; in others it was not. Father Chapdelaine went to Guangxi province, which was still officially closed to foreigners, to minister to a small group of Catholic converts in the town of Yaoshan. Chapdelaine was arrested on the orders of the local chief, badly beaten, and then left to die slowly in a small metal cage hung over the door of the local prison. After his death, his head was removed from his body and hung from a tree.

By the end of 1857, the British were still fighting the mutineers in India but managed to find sufficient troops to form a joint Anglo-French force which was assembled in Hong Kong. Sir Harry Parkes issued an ultimatum to the governor of Canton, Viceroy Ye Mingchen, threatening the occupation of Canton unless the remaining crew of the

Arrow were released. The three crewmen were eventually released, but Ye Mingchen offered no apology, and it was decided to go ahead with an invasion of Canton. The joint force arrived off Canton and proceeded to attack. A force of less than 6,000 troops seemed very little with which to overcome a city with one million inhabitants, but once again the superiority of weapons and tactics prevailed, and the city was taken at a total cost of 15 soldiers killed. Viceroy Ye Mingchen was captured and transported to India where he committed suicide by starving himself to death.

Anglo-French forces remained in control of Canton for almost four years. Part of the reason for the lack of a military response by the Chinese was an uprising which had broken out against the Qing dynasty. The Taiping Rebellion was led by Hong Xiuquan, a Chinese who had converted to Christianity and was determined to establish a Christian state in southern China. The Taiping Heavenly Kingdom began as a small movement, but it grew in power and popularity until Hong Xiuquan controlled a population of almost 30 million people. The Taiping Rebellion began in late 1850 and continued until 1864. It was not only the largest civil war ever to afflict China but also the bloodiest conflict of the nineteenth century. Estimates of casualties range from 20 to 70 million. In 1857, the Chinese emperor was fully committed to fighting this uprising, and troops simply could not be spared to fight the Anglo-French occupation of Canton.

In Britain, there was a great deal of unease about the *Arrow* incident and what seemed to many people as a disproportionate military response by British forces. The issue was raised in parliament and led to the passing of a motion of censure against the Whig Government. This prompted a General Election in March 1857. The Whigs, under Palmerston, claimed that their main opponents, the Tories, were being unpatriotic in not supporting British military action in China. The electorate agreed and Palmerston and the Whigs were returned with an increased majority. The new government agreed to support Sir Harry Parkes in demanding some form of restitution from the Chinese for the *Arrow* incident.

In May 1858, Anglo-French forces attacked and occupied the Taku Forts on the Hai River in Tianjin. In June, the Chinese, still fighting the Taiping Rebellion in the south, were forced to sign the Treaty of Tientsin which gave the British, French, Americans, and Russians the right to open embassies in Beijing (which had previously been closed to foreigners) and to open several more Chinese ports to trade with the West. China was also required to pay a large indemnity of four million taels of silver to Britain and two million to France. In return, the Taku Forts were returned to the Chinese.

It seemed that the Second Opium War was over, but in fact the signing of the Treaty of Tientsin marked only the end of its first phase.

Chapter Six

The Fall of Beijing

"Britain created the largest, most successful and most lucrative drug cartel the world had ever seen."

—Nicholas Saunders

Although the emperor had given permission for the negotiations which led to the signing of the Treaty of Tientsin, some of the terms of the treaty were not acceptable to the imperial court. In particular, the notion of allowing foreign embassies to be established in Beijing was felt to be too much—up to this time, foreigners had not been allowed to live in the imperial city. Responding to objections from some of his ministers, the Xianfeng Emperor decided that, although the treaty was signed and hostilities ended, it would not be ratified. Instead, China would use the resulting cease fire to build up its military forces, especially those based in the Taku Forts, to prevent further Western movement towards Beijing.

In 1858, further negotiations in Shanghai between the British and the Chinese agreed to the legalization of the opium trade. This was a significant concession as far as the British were concerned, but it seems that the Chinese had no more intention of honoring this agreement than they did the Treaty of Tientsin. In June 1859, British warships sailed north from Shanghai up to the mouth of the Hai River carrying British and French diplomats bound for Beijing. However, when they reached the Taku Forts, they were told that, while the diplomats might be permitted to continue by road to Beijing, they would not be allowed to be accompanied by troops or warships. The British ships attempted to force their way up the river, but they were fired upon from the forts. Three British gunboats were sunk, and three more ran aground. A force of Anglo-French troops attempted to take the forts but were repulsed in one of the few defeats suffered by the Western powers during the Opium Wars. In addition to the loss of three ships, the Anglo-French force lost almost 100 men killed and 350 wounded. The British fleet was forced to return to Shanghai.

Defeat in the Second Battle of the Taku Forts was a major blow to British military prestige. Up to this point, the British had seemed invincible, but their failure to take the forts made the Chinese imperial court believe that it might be possible to defeat the Westerners, and support for the continuation of the war grew in Beijing. However, the Indian Mutiny had ended in late 1858, and the British now had large numbers of troops available to be deployed in China. Sir Colin Campbell, the commander-in-chief of all forces in India, amassed a large force which was to be used for the next attempt to force a passage beyond the Taku Forts and on towards Beijing.

In the summer of 1860, an Anglo-French force of close to 18,000 men and 175 ships left Hong Kong bound for the Chinese ports of Yantai and Dalian. These were quickly captured, and the fleet sailed north, towards the mouth of the Hai River. On August 3, troops were landed at Beitang, a short distance from the Taku Forts. After stiff fighting, the last fort was captured on August 21. The Anglo-French army then took the city of Tianjin on August 23 and began to march inland, towards Beijing.

Alarmed by the loss of the Taku Forts and Tianjin, the Chinese emperor sent ministers to discuss peace terms with the Anglo-French. Sir Harry Parkes and a group of envoys accompanied by journalists from British and French newspapers met with the Chinese representatives in early September. However, after an allegation that Parkes had insulted one of the imperial representatives, the whole Anglo-French delegation was arrested on September 18 and taken to Beijing. All were interrogated and twenty people, including two British envoys and a journalist for *The Times* newspaper, were eventually executed. They were killed by a method known as slow slicing, a particularly horrible method of execution which involved keeping the victim alive as long as possible while severing parts of the body. When the mutilated and virtually unrecognizable bodies of those who had been killed in this way were returned to the Anglo-French army, there was outrage and a desire for retribution. Sir Parkes and the surviving members of the delegation continued to be held in captivity.

Also on September 18, Anglo-French troops fought with the troops of the Chinese commander in charge of the defense of Beijing, Mongol General Sengge Rinchen. The Chinese troops proved unable to stop or even to significantly slow the advancing Western army, and Sengge Rinchen withdrew to Palikao (Eight Mile Bridge) on the outskirts of Beijing where he prepared defensive positions. Rinchen commanded over 10,000 men including a large contingent of elite Mongol cavalry, and he was confident in his ability to defeat the smaller Western army.

The climactic battle of the Second Opium War took place on the morning of September 21, 1860. The Chinese army was well established in front of a canal which connected Beijing and the Peiho River, near two large stone bridges at Palikao. The Anglo-French force arrived in the evening of the 20th and took up positions opposite the Chinese forces. On the morning of the 21st, Sengge Rinchen launched the first of a series of massive frontal attacks on the Anglo-French positions, led by his Mongol cavalry and supported by waves of infantry.

Facing some of the best trained and equipped European troops, the Chinese weren't just defeated, their army was virtually annihilated. Unable to retreat because of the canal behind them, units were forced to fight until they were wiped out. By the afternoon of September 21, Beijing was left without any effective defensive force. The Xianfeng Emperor immediately fled, first to the Imperial Summer Palace in the mountains of Chengde and then on to Rehe province. He left his brother, Prince Gong, in charge of Beijing and responsible for negotiations with the Anglo-French.

With the defeat of the defenders, the Anglo-French army quickly began preparations for the storming of Beijing. Engineers built entrenched positions for artillery batteries and prepared methods of breaking through the city's huge walls. Then, on October 8, just as the assault was ready to begin, the city gates were opened, and Beijing surrendered to the Anglo-French force. Sir Parkes and the other surviving members of the delegation were released unharmed.

The person in charge of the Anglo-French forces was James Bruce, 8th Earl of Elgin and British high commissioner and plenipotentiary in China and the Far East. Lord Elgin was faced with the decision of what to do in order to punish the Chinese for the torture and execution of the envoys. Initially, he favored burning the Forbidden City, the vast imperial palace complex in the heart of Beijing. This site comprised almost 1,000 buildings spread over almost 200 acres. Elgin believed that the destruction of Forbidden City, one of the most revered sites in China, would send an appropriate message to the emperor to dissuade him from ordering the execution of any more Western envoys. However, the French believed that this might be counter-productive in that it would constitute such an affront to the imperial dynasty that it might prevent them from signing a peace treaty. Instead, Elgin agreed to the burning of the Yiheyuan (the Summer Palace) and the Yuanmingyuan (the Old Summer Palace).

These two palaces were places of great antiquity and architectural interest, and both were packed with artwork and treasure. Nevertheless, they were thoroughly looted of all their treasures before being burned to the ground on October 18, 1860. On the same day, Prince Gong ratified the Treaty of Tientsin during what has become known as the Convention of Beijing, bringing the Second Opium War officially to an end.

The Convention of Beijing included an agreement by China to pay an indemnity of eight million taels of silver to Britain and France, the ceding of Kowloon (a large port close to Hong Kong) to the British, and granting Christians throughout China the right to own property and to evangelize without restriction. Most importantly to Britain, the opium trade was legalized. With the ratification of the treaty, the British had achieved everything they had set out to do in China.

Chapter Seven

Aftermath

"Beyond a doubt, by 1860 the ancient civilization that was China had been thoroughly defeated and humiliated by the West."

— Immanuel Chung-Yueh Hsü

In Britain, the defeat of China and the subsequent Convention of Beijing were seen as a great victory and in particular as a triumph for Lord Palmerston, who became even more popular than before. British merchants took advantage of the opening of trade with China to establish even more lucrative trading routes which included the now legal selling of opium. But not everyone in Britain was delighted at the outcome of the war. British Chancellor of the Exchequer William Ewart Gladstone was a particularly vociferous opponent of the Opium Wars and the British trade in opium in general. Gladstone, who would go on to be leader of the new Liberal Party and British prime minister in 1868, referred to the wars as "Palmerston's Opium Wars" and said that he lived "in dread of the judgments of God upon England for our national iniquity towards China."

Despite growing concern in Britain about the morality of the opium trade with China, it continued for many years after the end of the war. In the end, it wasn't moral outrage that caused the opium trade with China to decrease—it was the increasing cultivation of poppies and the domestic production of opium within China. By 1884, a British journalist would write: "We English, by the policy we have pursued, are morally responsible for every acre of land in China which is withdrawn from the cultivation of grain and devoted to that of the poppy; so that the fact of the growth of the drug in China ought only to increase our sense of responsibility."

The British export of opium from India to China did not finally end until the fall of the Qing government in 1912, but by that time domestic production of opium was more than capable of keeping up with demand. Opium addiction continued to be a major problem in China up until Mao Zedong's communist revolution led to the establishment of the People's Republic of China in 1949. Under Mao's leadership, opium addiction was substantially reduced by forcing more than ten million known addicts to accept often brutal and arbitrary treatment and by the execution of thousands of dealers. Despite these measures, it was estimated in 2003 that China still had two million regular opium users and one million registered addicts. All can be traced directly back to the British trade in Opium and the Chinese defeat in the First and Second Opium Wars.

The Xianfeng Emperor died on August 22, 1861, in his Summer Palace in Chengde. He was succeeded by his six-year-old son, Zaichun, but his brother Prince Gong was appointed regent and became the de-facto leader of China. Humiliating military defeats in the Opium Wars and the continuing effects of the Taiping Rebellion (which would not end until 1864) left Imperial China in a seriously weakened state. It was clear that Chinese military forces were not able to fight their Western counterparts on equal terms. This led to the creation of what became known as the Self-Strengthening Movement. One of the most influential figures behind this movement was the respected scholar Feng Guifen who wrote several essays in the period immediately following the end of the Second Opium War. These considered what the Chinese needed to do to improve their military capabilities to the point where they could fight successfully against the West. In one essay, *On the Manufacture of Foreign Weapons*, Feng wrote: "What we have to learn from the barbarians is only the one thing—solid ships and effective guns."

For more than 30 years the Qing dynasty adopted the suggestion made by Feng and other members of the movement. New dockyards and arsenals were created using Western technology to build ship and weapons that were at least equal to those used by Western armies. Training was also addressed, and thousands of naval and military cadets were sent for training in academies in Britain, France, and Germany. These cadets brought back to China knowledge of the latest military strategy and tactics, and these were in turn incorporated in training in Chinese military and naval training establishments. By the late 1880s, the Chinese Beiyang Fleet was equipped with modern ships and was the largest naval unit in Asia and the eighth largest military fleet in the world.

In 1894, the modernized Chinese army and navy were tested for the first time when the First Sino-Japanese war broke out. Japan, like China, had been intent on improving its military and naval units since the beginning of the Meiji

Restoration in the late 1860s. By 1894, Japan was beginning to challenge China as the dominant Asian power, and war broke out over control of the Korean Peninsula. Despite improvements in its military and naval forces, this war proved as disastrous for the Chinese as the Opium Wars had been. After ten months of unbroken defeats on sea and land, China sued for peace and handed control of Korea to Japan. This marked an important shift in power in Asia and represented a major loss of prestige to the Qing dynasty. This led directly to the Xinhai Revolution of 1911 and the abdication of China's last emperor the following year. After 2,000 years of imperial rule and a position as a major world power, China entered the modern era in 1912 with the formation of the Republic of China.

Conclusion

The scale and scope of China's defeat in the Opium Wars surprised even the victors, Britain and France, who obtained everything they had hoped for from these wars. Victory in these wars bolstered British trade and increased support for the belligerent British Palmerston government which encouraged further British imperial expansion.

In stark contrast, the consistent defeats suffered by the best military units possessed by the Chinese led to an erosion of respect for the Qing dynasty. Partly, these defeats were due to the inferior equipment and training of Chinese military and naval units, but the prosecution of the war was also hampered by the consistent unwillingness of local governors or military commanders to report defeats. Even the most abject failure was often reported as a victory, which gave the Chinese high command located in the distant imperial court of Beijing a false picture of how the war was progressing.

The combination of defeat in the First and Second Opium Wars and the continuing Taiping Rebellion undermined a dynasty that had ruled China for 2,000 years. For almost the first time, growing numbers of Chinese people began to question whether Imperial China had become so weak that it could no longer protect its interests; it was a short step to open rebellion and the establishment 50 years later of a Chinese Republic

In the 1850s, China still appeared to most outsiders to be a significant world power and the leading nation in Asia. Within ten years the Opium Wars had helped to expose the reality: that a corrupt, distant leadership no longer commanded military forces capable of resisting foreign incursion or even of preventing the importation of narcotics that addicted million of its people. The internal turmoil triggered by the Opium Wars led directly to the fall of an empire and the creation of modern China.

Made in the USA
Coppell, TX
06 February 2022

73018098R00026